the little book of

CACTI

and other succulents

emma sibley

photography by adam laycock

Hardie Grant

QUADRILLE

I would love to dedicate this book to my grandparents, Ben and Ethel Howard, for passing on their green fingers to me.

Contents

Introduction

WHAT ARE CACTI AND SUCCULENTS?

Cacti and succulents are plants that can store water in their leaves and stems, which allows them to survive in very dry places. All cacti are succulents; cacti have areoles – small, round, cushion-like bumps from which spines grow – but succulents have none.

These hardy plants have been part of the horticultural scene for a long time, but they have become increasingly popular with urban gardeners and green-fingered city dwellers in the past few years.

Today there is a greater choice of houseplants than ever before in specialist stores, garden centres and florists, with a wide variety of cacti and succulents to pick from. We have, however, become accustomed to seeing the Organ Pipe and Prickly Pear Cactus in Hollywood films, but there are many more forms with globular bodies and unusual leaf shapes and textures, such as the hanging Fishbone and Pencil Cacti.

There is a common belief that these low-maintenance plants can survive all forms of neglect, but this is not always true. This book aims to describe a selection of some of the better-known cacti and succulents, as well as more obscure and hard-to-find ones. It will also shed some light on the best watering habits, where to position your plants, and how to deal with any problems that may occur.

HOW TO USE THIS BOOK

Each plant entry includes key information about caring for that particular variety. All the information is clearly organized under appropriate symbols which will help you give your plants everything they need to grow and thrive.

KEY TO SYMBOLS

LIGHT

WATER

GROWTH AND CARE

POTTING

FLOWERS

PRUNING

PROPAGATION

WATCH OUT FOR

QUIRKS

DID YOU KNOW

Each plant is given its common and Latin name; occasionally these are the same. The Latin or botanical name provides information about the relationship between plants and is known as the taxonomic status. All plants belong to a particular family and these are divided into *genera* (the plural of *genus*). The Latin name of each plant consists of two words; the *genus* and the species. The *genus* is a collective name for a group of plants, and the species (or specific epithet) tells you more about a particular plant.

How to start a collection

BUYING YOUR PLANTS

———

I believe that after purchasing your first prickly friend, the decision to start a collection of cacti and succulents is almost taken out of your hands. An addiction to these plants seems to take hold.

You can purchase cacti and succulents almost anywhere; local florists, online growers and specialist stores are all ideal places to begin your hunt. Don't be afraid to ask if you want something in particular to grow your collection.

The succulents and cacti you can pick up from your local garden centre are often growing in small, solitary pots containing one or two rosettes, so the opportunity to pick up a few of these at a time and grow them together is a joy in itself.

How often do you see a cactus or succulent standing lonesome on a window ledge? They are almost always accompanied by a second or third potted friend.

HANDY TIPS

When choosing your plants, consider the health of the plant. Watch out for scarring, dying leaves, root rot, damage or discolouration. Most importantly, make sure your plant doesn't have any bugs or diseases. Don't fall into the trap of feeling sorry for a plant because you will end up having to do more work to try to revive it.

Potting and tools

CLAY OR CONCRETE POTS

These are ideal for cacti and succulents because the walls are porous and allow excess water through. Plants are usually sold in plastic pots, which are less attractive than clay pots, but do help the plants retain moisture.

WATERING

It is always handy to have a watering can to make the task of hydrating/feeding your plants fun. You'll find some plants prefer to be watered with a mister.

COMPOST AND GRAVEL

Most collectors have their own recipe for the ideal compost mix; however it is perfectly acceptable to pick up ready-mixed cacti and succulent compost in your local garden centre. This is a sandy and gritty mixture that allows good drainage for the roots. Ensure that the compost you use is loose and aerated, even when wet, to prevent waterlogging and root rot. You will need to put a layer of gravel or small stones in the bottom of each pot to help with drainage.

OTHER TOOLS

Trowels come in a range of sizes and are useful for mixing soil and repotting plants. Buy a sturdy pair of gardening gloves; without these repotting can be a painfully prickly business! A small pair of cactus grippers or tweezers is also useful for pruning and propagating your plant.

Propagation

PROPAGATION IS THE PROCESS OF
CREATING NEW PLANTS FROM A
CUTTING, AN OFFSET OR A SEED.

Once you are the owner of a cactus or succulent you will be able
to start creating your own collection. Propagation can be done in
several ways; the most popular ways are taking cuttings and raising
plants from seed.

CUTTINGS

Many cacti and succulents produce pups or offsets (small versions of
themselves) in the first few years of growth. These can be removed
from the parent plant, rooted and then repotted. You can remove one
of the fleshy leaves of a plant such as a Houseleek or Burro's Tail very
easily without damaging the rest of the plant. If you place this leaf
on a bed of dry, gritty soil you will soon notice that the cut surface
dries and hardens, forming a callus; shortly afterwards it will start
to root. When rooting, keep cuttings in light shade to prevent them
shrivelling. Small plantlets should begin to sprout from the base of the
original leaf, which means it can then be planted. The original leaf will
eventually die back, leaving room for the new plant to grow.

GROWING FROM THE SEED

You can buy cactus and succulent seed from garden centres or online. Raising plants from seed is perhaps one of the most rewarding ways to propagate. Although this may be a longer process than taking cuttings, you will be able to watch every stage of your plants' growth.

Gather a collection of small pots filled with moist, sterile potting soil. Distribute the seeds between the pots, allowing space between the seeds for each plant to grow. Scatter some compost over the seeds, but do not press down and compact it; shoots will push up through it. Keep the pots in a warm and humid place to help germination; the compost should be kept moist and in light shade. When the seeds start to germinate and a tiny plant appears, transfer it into a more gritty porous compost so the plant can grow to maturity.

Troubleshooting

OVERWATERING

Possibly the most troublesome part of owning a cactus or succulent is knowing how often to water it. Overwatering is one of the easiest ways to damage a plant and can often have fatal results.

As desert plants, cacti and succulents thrive in arid environments. Their bulbous leaves or stems have adapted to store the water the plants need to survive drought. You should try to replicate their natural conditions at home.

During the warmer summer months when the plants are growing, water them once a week. Decrease watering during winter dormancy – some plants should be kept completely dry through the cool winter months in order to avoid root rot. However, some groups of cacti and succulents have reverse growing patterns. These plants should be watered very little in the summer but more during winter when they are growing.

Signs of overwatering include wilting or mushy roots and stems, with healthy leaves dropping off. If this happens you may be able to save your plant by repotting it. Gently lift the plant out of the pot and remove as much soil as possible from the roots without breaking them. Cut off any rotting or damaged roots. Then fill a clean pot with compost (not all the way to the top of the pot) and place your plant in the centre, spreading out the roots before covering them with soil until the plant is held securely on the surface.

BURNING

Scorching can also be a problem with many cacti and succulents. Placing them in direct sunshine beside a window can be detrimental. Scorching shows as brown marks on the leaves or body of the plant. If this happens move your plant into indirect sun or light shade to prevent further damage.

PESTS

Pests can also be a threat to your cacti and succulents, particularly mealy bugs, which you may notice in the growing creases of various succulents – they look a bit like a mass of sticky cotton wool. One way to prevent pests setting up home in and around your plant is to remove any wilting leaves or dead matter that has accumulated in the pot below, as these provide the perfect environment for mealy bugs and spider mites to thrive.

NO GROWTH

If you have had a plant for a while and have noticed no signs of growth, this could be caused by a number of things. It could be due to underwatering in the summer or overwatering in the winter. Another possible cause is stunted growth which can happen when you haven't repotted your plant for a long time. Plants should ideally be repotted as they grow. If a plant is not repotted its roots can become cramped and pot-bound.

SHEDDING

If your plant seems to be shedding a lot of leaves this could be an indication that the temperature is too high or that you are underwatering. It is important to be aware that shedding is a natural process in which plants self-propagate. If you are concerned then try moving your plant to a new location.

Cacti

AND OTHER SUCCULENTS

———

A large barrel cactus with multiple hooked spines, one of which is almost always flattened, the Twisted Barrel originated in the Mexican desert. Usually a solitary plant, it does not often form clumps.

Twisted Barrel Cactus

FEROCACTUS HERRERAE

WATER:

In the desert, the Twisted Barrel is used to having two months of continuous rain followed by drought and plenty of sunlight. During the summer growing period make sure that you water well in free-draining soil, and be sure not to get any water on the body of the cactus as this can cause burning and sometimes scarring if the plant is in direct sunlight. During the winter months keep the plant dry.

FLOWERS:

The flowers are always yellow with a red centre and are produced from late summer until early autumn.

PROPAGATION:

Seeds are the only way of propagating this cactus; in the past these seeds have also been ground and used to make flour.

DID YOU KNOW:

This aggressive looking cactus produces cream/purple blooms which can attract butterflies and bees, if kept outside. It is also known to produce edible fruits.

Native to southern Mexico, the Burro's Tail, adorned with fleshy, blue-green leaves and pink flowers in summer, is a favourite trailing succulent in the home.

Burro's Tail SEDUM MORGANIANUM

LIGHT:

Grown indoors or out, the Burro's Tail will revel in full sunlight – the more exposure the plant has to bright light, the stronger the leaves become and the more enhanced the leaf colour will be. Inside the Burro's Tail is quite a pale plant; however, if you're lucky to see it in its native Mexico, you will notice the greater intensity of the leaf colour.

WATER:

This plant is quite susceptible to overwatering, so be cautious during the winter months and water only once every few weeks. For the remainder of the year the Burro's Tail will appreciate moderate watering as long as there is good drainage to allow the soil to dry out.

PROPAGATION:

One of the easiest succulents to propagate and possibly the most satisfying plants to watch grow. Gently remove some leaves from the plant, lay them on soil until the ends callous over and they can be planted.

WATCH OUT FOR:

Please be extra careful when handling the Burro's Tail, as the leaves are incredibly fragile and fall off at the slightest knock.

These miniature aloe-like plants have become increasingly popular due to their attractive zebra stripes and tolerance of neglect. Native to South Africa, they grow as solitary plants or clump together, depending on the type of soil they are growing in.

Zebra Cactus HAWORTHIA ATTENUATA

WATER:

The Zebra Cactus is very tolerant of underwatering but should be watered about once every two weeks in the summer. However, it is also very susceptible to overwatering, and this can easily promote root rot.

POTTING:

Zebra Cacti look great in brightly coloured or striped pots and containers. It is even possible to use different sand mixes on top of the soil to make the most of their distinctive patterns.

FLOWERS:

The plants will produce flowers annually, usually just after the longest day of the year. These flowers are not the most exciting blooms, due to the dormant nature of the *Haworthia* throughout the year, but flowering is a great signifier that your plant is doing well.

PROPAGATION:

The Zebra Cacti can be propagated in the same way as Aloe plants. Cut off a bit of a leaf and let the wound heal over, allowing the leaf to dry out. Alternatively, this plant produces offsets that can be removed and replanted.

Perhaps one of the most interesting-looking succulent plants, the Buddha's Temple has a distinguishing leaf formation. Extremely tightly packed, the silvery green leaves branch out in sets of four and then fold up at the edges, forming an almost perfectly square column. You may also notice a white powdery residue on the surface; this develops to help preserve moisture and protect the plant from strong sunlight.

Buddha's Temple

CRASSULA 'BUDDHA'S TEMPLE'

LIGHT:

Giving the Buddah's Temple plenty of sunlight will help to keep the leaves compact and promote strong coloured flowers. Try not to expose the plant to direct sunlight in summer, however, as this may prove too strong.

FLOWERS:

Flowers may appear at any point throughout the year, when the conditions are right. When flowers do appear, you will see bright-red and orange blooms branching out from the top of the plant.

PRUNING:

A well-cared-for Buddha's Temple may grow to a height of 15cm (6in) tall. At this point you will notice that extra stems will start branching out from the sides of the column. After many years the plant may start to look untidy and straggly, so it is a good idea to cut the stem down almost to the root to encourage new growth.

You will find the Beehive Cactus residing in the desert scrub of its native Mexico or in the conifer forests of Canada, high up in the mountains. This solitary cactus may sometimes clump to form beds of small bodies, each covered in a web of aggressive looking star-shaped spines.

Beehive Cactus

ESCOBARIA VIVIPARA

LIGHT: Ensuring that this cactus is exposed to full sun in the morning to light shade throughout the day will promote strong growth and increase the chance of blooming. The Beehive is known for producing vivid fuchsia-coloured flowers during spring to late summer.

WATER: The Beehive originates from an area with summer rainfall, so water it moderately once a week throughout the warmer months (April to early September) ensuring that the compost dries out completely between waterings to prevent root rot. Through the cooler winter months reduce watering to once every two to three weeks.

PROPAGATION: Propagation can be achieved through cuttings. You can take off the head of the Beehive and leave it to callus over until dry, then replant it in a gritty, sandy compost to root.

A fast-growing plant native to South Africa and part of the stacked *Crassula* genus, the leaves of the String of Buttons grow on top of each other, with the stem running directly through the middle of each leaf. Although it seems to grow in separate stems, the String of Buttons is somewhat shrubby, branching off in all directions.

String of Buttons

CRASSULA PERFORATA 'VARIEGATA'

LIGHT:

The String of Buttons flourishes in indirect sunlight or light shade. Avoid direct sunlight, as this may burn the plant's leaves; however, brighter light will bring out luscious red tones on the leaf tips.

GROWTH AND CARE:

This fast-growing succulent can grow as tall as 46cm (18in) with leaves 2.5cm (1in) long. Although these plants are easy to grow they are extremely susceptible to mealy bugs and fungal diseases. If you do discover an infestation of mealy bugs then you can make a simple soap spray. Mix 1 litre (4 cups) water with ¼ tsp of washing-up liquid and apply the solution by gently spraying the affected areas. Start by testing a small area to see whether the plant reacts to the solution.

POTTING:

Due to its creeping nature, your String of Buttons may need repotting every year or two. Make sure the compost is completely dry and repot in a gritty well draining mix.

A tall, columnar cactus that is usually not any wider than its container, the *Euphorbia acrurensis* can reach heights of up to 3m (10ft).

Desert Candle

EUPHORBIA ACRURENSIS

LIGHT:

In its native South Africa, this cactus receives maximum sunlight in its arid desert environment; this should be mirrored as much as possible in the home. It may be a good idea to place the Desert Candle near a window, but watch out for burns if it is in direct sunlight.

WATER:

When watering, these large plants need their soil to be completely soaked through once a week during the summer. As with most cacti, make sure the soil is completely dry between waterings, also that stagnant water does not collect in the bottom of the pot.

WATCH OUT FOR:

Euphorbias typically produce a white, milky sap called latex which can cause skin irritation when touched. This plant is also moderately poisonous to cats and dogs.

QUIRKS:

The Desert Candle will grow small, delicate leaves near the top of its stems. These appear to be hanging on only by a thread and can be easily knocked off, but it is perfectly normal for these to be shed every year and then replaced by new ones.

Although it creeps along the ground in its indigenous South Africa, *Senecio mandraliscae* is perfect for larger pots and hanging baskets in the home. Perhaps the bluest cactus around, the beauty of this plant lies in the colour of its leaves.

Blue Chalk Sticks

SENECIO MANDRALISCAE

LIGHT: Blue Chalk Sticks is used to partial sunlight, growing in shady patches along the desert floor, so will be happy in indirect sunlight in your home.

WATER: Because it copes very well with drought, the Blue Chalk Sticks will survive many weeks without watering, although if you pot it in well-drained soil and give it a weekly watering you will quickly see the benefits. Be sure to keep it in a well-ventilated room, as too much humidity can cause the plant to rot.

POTTING: With its small bunching stems, this plant will thrive both outdoors and in. If you do put your plant outside, plant it in a moveable pot so you can bring in before the frost.

PRUNING: The Blue Chalk Sticks can grow up to 46cm (18in) tall and 61cm (24in) wide. You may find that the stems tend to flop over; if this happens prune back each stem to where it feels firm. You can then replant the cuttings in damp, sandy soil where they will take root.

Resembling a sea creature rather than a desert plant, the Curly Locks is known for its aquatic sea-green leaves with frilly, pale-pink tips. Unlike many other *Echeverias* the Curly Locks has a very relaxed rosette. Although a very slow-growing plant, after many years it can spread up to 25cm (10in) in diameter and grow to be 30cm (12in) high.

 *Echeveria* CURLY LOCKS

LIGHT: Enjoying the sun, Curly Locks will be happy sitting on a windowsill with plenty of natural light, but it will also appreciate the occasional shady spot.

WATER: During the summer, make sure to water it well once a week, and be careful not to get water on the leaf pads, as this can cause discolouration and kill the leaves. During the winter, water much less frequently: once every few weeks and only enough to prevent the leaves from shrivelling.

FLOWERS: Flowering takes place from April to late September. If your Curly Locks does flower you will have a collection of bright orange-red blooms.

PROPAGATION: Because this plant is very slow to offset, it is much quicker to propagate via a leaf cutting. Set the cutting aside on some dry soil until the end dries out completely, then plant it in some free-draining, gritty compost.

Found on the cliffs of Mexico, the *Mammillaria backebergiana* is an attractive columnar cactus with a dense covering of yellow-white spines and purple-pink flowers that bloom throughout the summer months. As it grows quickly in clumps, you may need to repot your cactus every few years to give it room to grow and develop.

MAMMILLARIA BACKEBERGIANA

LIGHT: The *backebergiana* copes in direct sunshine. Exposing it to four or five hours of light every day will promote flowering and increase the strength of the spines. A few hours of shade are also good during intense summer sun.

WATER: Watering should be kept to a minimum. Throughout the summer water moderately every week, ensuring that the compost is fully dry between waterings. Winter watering should be decreased to once every two to three weeks.

FLOWERS: If the conditions are right, the *backebergiana* will bloom several times throughout the summer. The pink flowers appear in rings around the crown.

WATCH OUT FOR: Do not allow water to rest between the spines as this can cause rotting and discolouring of the plant's body.

Native to the dry, rocky regions of South Africa and Madagascar, the Aloe Vera is one of the most popular aloes kept in the home.

ALOE VERA

LIGHT:
Used to living in a harsh, dry environment under bushes, the Aloe vera does not need much natural light and is a relatively hardy plant to keep, although it will appreciate a dry, south-facing room.

WATER:
Take care when watering, as water on the leaves can cause rotting and watering when the plant is dormant during the winter can cause root rot. Allow the soil to dry out completely between waterings.

POTTING:
Use a terracotta pot, as the porous material soaks up any excess moisture from the compost.

WATCH OUT FOR:
Be careful if you have a curious cat or dog as this plant is mildly toxic to pets and is known to cause vomiting if ingested.

DID YOU KNOW:
Clear aloe vera sap has been used for centuries to treat minor burns and skin irritations, making it the perfect plant to keep on your kitchen windowsill in case of burns.

A very decorative jungle cactus, you will find this epiphytic plant hanging from the trees in Bolivia and other areas of South America. At home, this cactus will be happy in a hanging basket or on a shelf that allows its limbs room to grow without cramping.

LEPISMIUM BOLIVIANUM

LIGHT: As you would expect from a jungle plant, the *Lepismium bolivianum* will thrive in the shade; however, occasional exposure to sunlight will strengthen the plant and encourage flowering.

WATER: This cactus appreciates being kept damp, so use a mister to spray it once a week. Add a little water to the compost once every two weeks, but do not allow the roots to sit in damp soil, as this can prove fatal.

FLOWERS: Flowering usually occurs throughout the summer months. Bright orange-pink blooms appear along the edges of the stems, and these may last for a few weeks.

PROPAGATION: Relatively easy to propagate from a cutting, you can root the *Lepismium* in a gritty soil mixture in a few short weeks. Make sure that you keep the root and soil dry until roots have formed; otherwise the cutting may rot.

A fast-growing epiphytic plant found growing in the angles of trees and on rock faces in Brazil, the stems of the Bottle Cactus start out pointed and erect but droop under their own weight as they have neither spines or a central stem. A perfect plant to pop in a hanging basket, the Bottle Cactus will also grow tall in a pot with the help of a few supporting sticks.

Bottle Cactus HATIORA SALICORNIOIDES

LIGHT:

This cactus struggles in direct sunlight, but will enjoy a free-draining pot placed in a cool, shady area of the home. Plenty of sunlight is needed for growth and production of flowers, but the Bottle Cactus will be much happier in full shade.

FLOWERS:

The tiny bright-orange flowers contrast beautifully with the green of the stems. These then develop into translucent green berries with a reddish tip.

PROPAGATION:

Self-propagating, any offset stems will easily root to form a new plant. This may overgrow the original plant in time.

DID YOU KNOW:

The name Bottle Cactus comes from the small segments of the stems that seem to resemble tiny upside-down beer bottles. These small, droopy stems are bright green in colour and sometimes speckled with a purple haze. The Bottle Cactus is also known as Dancing Bones and Spice Cactus.

A bright-green cactus with very straight, columnar trunks, for centuries the columns of the Mexican Fence Post have been grown shoulder to shoulder and used as fences to keep cattle on their pastures.

Mexican Fence Post Cactus

PACHYCEREUS MARGINATUS

LIGHT: Sunny conditions are advisable. This cactus is used to living in very dry conditions so it will enjoy as much sunlight as possible.

WATER: Mexican Fence Posts can be left untouched for years; they are very durable and hardly need any watering at all. To keep them in their best condition, water them once a week during the hotter summer months, but allow the soil to dry out completely before watering again. During the winter, they need even less water, so only add some once every few weeks.

POTTING: As these cacti can grow to great heights of 6.1m (20ft) tall, repotting must be done with caution. The plant can become top-heavy, so you may need to repot once every few years to replace the soil and increase the pot size. After repotting, allow the cactus to stand for a few weeks before watering it again so that the roots can establish themselves and the cactus doesn't topple out.

Native to South Africa, this small succulent is known for its tightly packed leaves that all grow around a thin stem, forming a square mass. Many of these stems grow together in a bushy formation up to 20cm (8in) in length, so this is a perfect houseplant for a hanging basket where its limbs can hang and grow freely.

Watch Chain

CRASSULA LYCOPODIOIDES

LIGHT:

Favouring a room with bright sunlight and perhaps even some early morning direct sun, the Watch Chain will thrive in the heat, as long as the humidity is low.

WATER:

Water abundantly in summer soaking the soil, but be sure to remove any water from the tray and allow the pot to dry out completely before watering again. During the winter months, if the plant is in a cool place, do not water or feed at all; resume when the cactus is in a warmer temperature.

FLOWERS:

A cool winter location can also encourage a bloom in the spring. You will notice small yellow flowers growing from the stems of the plant, and these can sometimes smell quite pungent and unpleasant, so be aware!

PROPAGATION:

The Watch Chain is generally started by offsets or leaf cuttings, making them incredibly easy to propagate from a single leaf. Leave your cuttings to sprout, then plant in a succulent or cacti soil mix.

Native to Florida – hence their Latin name – these cacti are quite rare due to the fact that they only bloom throughout the night. In their natural habitat the flowers appear after the sun has gone down and they only ever last one night.

Night-flowering Cactus

CEREUS FLORIDA

LIGHT: The Night-flowering Cactus will thrive in plenty of sunlight but also enjoy the odd bit of shade as well, so do not place in direct sunlight as this may cause scalding of the plant's skin.

WATER: During the summer months, water well once a week but then wait until the soil has completely dried out before watering again. Throughout the winter, when temperatures are much cooler, your cactus may become dormant. In this period water sparingly: as little as every few weeks. The Cereus florida will have stored copious amounts of water in its limbs to survive during this time.

POTTING: The Cereus florida performs well in unglazed ceramics and terracotta pots. It is important that this plant has a porous pot as the weight of the pot provides stability.

DID YOU KNOW: ? The fruits produced after flowerings are edible raw. They are from the same family as the dragon fruit.

Probably one of the most popular succulents in the home, this *Crassula* is native to South Africa and grows as a small tree or shrub in its natural habitat. With small, round, egg-shaped leaves – from which the name Money Tree is derived – the plant will produce pinkish-white flowers when it blooms once a year.

Money Tree  CRASSULA OVATA

LIGHT:

The Money Tree grows best in natural sunlight. However, it is very tolerant of low light and lack of water, so the Money Tree will survive without a lot of attention.

GROWTH AND CARE:

The Money Tree can grow to be quite large and you may need to repot it every few years. Make sure the soil is completely dry before handling the plant, as wet soil can be detrimental to continuing growth.

POTTING:

This plant will be content to stay in the same pot for years so it doesn't need frequent repotting, but every couple of years or so it is good to change the soil otherwise it can get stale. Try to do this in the spring and avoid watering until you see signs of new growth.

PROPAGATION:

It's very easy to propagate the Money Tree, as new plants will grow easily from stem cuttings or even single leaves. Leave a leaf to crisp over on dry compost until it starts to root and you will have a new Money Tree within a few months.

Native to the desert hillsides of the Canary Islands, the Tree Houseleek's woody stems branch out in all directions, allowing their green or red rosettes to catch as much sun as possible.

Tree Houseleek  AEONIUM ARBOREUM

LIGHT:

In the home be sure to give your *Aeonium* as much sun as possible to help it keep its circular shape. This will prevent the leaves curling up.

WATER:

Care should be taken with Tree Houseleeks to prevent overwatering. During the summer months they should be watered and then left until the soil is lightly damp; however, during the winter months leave the compost until it is fully dry before watering again.

POTTING:

These plants are very fast growing and may need repotting once a year. They can grow to 1.5m (5ft) tall so to secure your plant as it grows, pot it in a sandy soil mix.

FLOWERS:

You may see small, star-like yellow flowers blooming from the centre of the rosettes from late winter to early spring. Be aware, though, that after flowering the rosette will die off.

QUIRKS:

Because of the speed of growth and weight of the rosettes, occasionally some of the branches may snap off. However, these can be used later for propagation.

Regularly grown for its furry, velvet-like leaves, the Panda Plant is relatively easy to care for, storing much of its water in its thick, succulent leaves. A light grey-green in colour, the tips of the leaves develop a brown spotting with maturity; their shape can also become quite irregular with time, but they usually start off as ovals. Originally from Madagascar, this pretty plant can grow up to 46cm (18in) tall.

Panda Plant

KALANCHOE TOMENTOSA

LIGHT:
This plant enjoys plenty of sunlight, so place it in a conservatory or bright living room to encourage strong new growth.

POTTING:
Once the Panda Plant is mature and the stems start to grow down below the pot, it is perfect to pot in a hanging basket. As a slow grower the Panda Plant may only need repotting once every few years, then even less when it has hit maturity.

FLOWERS:
Although the Panda Plant flowers in the wild, this is very rare in the home. However, the beauty of the leaves alone make it a firm household favourite.

WATCH OUT FOR:
Beware if you have any household pets as *Kalanchoe* are toxic to both dogs and cats

Native to the Americas and Mexico the Fishhook Cactus favours the arid conditions of the desert, so take this into account when potting. Use a deep pot to accommodate all the plant's roots and make sure the soil is gritty and free-draining.

Fishhook Cactus

ANCISTROCACTUS MEGARHIZUS

LIGHT:

Because they need a lot of sun, Fishhooks become quite stressed in low light, and this may lead to poor growth and weakening of the spines. Your *Ancistrocactus* will be happy on an airy kitchen windowsill that gets plenty of natural light but also shade every now and again. Alternatively, if you have a greenhouse it will be at home in there.

WATER:

During the winter months this cactus will tolerate cooler temperatures; just make sure that watering is kept to a minimum during this time, and allow the soil to dry out fully between waterings.

FLOWERS:

If the Fishhook is happy and has the right conditions, it will flower readily from February to March, producing bright-green to yellow blooms.

GROWTH AND CARE:

This desert cactus loves a sandy soil with a little topsoil and compost. Prepared cacti soil mixes also work just fine.

With its beautifully smooth, soup-plate-sized leaves, the Paddle Plant grows in a rosette shape, with its green leaves gaining red rims when exposed to sunlight. When grown in pairs, the leaves almost resemble lips.

Paddle Plant

KALANCHOE THYRSIFLORA

WATER:
This South African succulent grows freely in the desert, so it does well in dry homes. It needs only minimal watering once a week and even less in the winter months.

POTTING:
You may need to repot your Paddle Plant if it becomes crowded. However make sure that the compost is completely dry and use a pot that is only slightly larger than the previous one.

FLOWERS:
In the spring, mature plants produce fragrant yellow blooms. After flowering the plant forms buds that can be propagated.

WATCH OUT FOR:
The *Kalanchoe* species are toxic to animals. Take care if you have a household pet such as a dog or cat as this plant can be poisonous to these animals, if ingested.

DID YOU KNOW:
The Paddle Plant is also known as the Red Pancakes, Flap Jack and Desert Cabbage. This slow-growing plant does not require a lot of care to grow and thrive.

Often used as a natural fencing in its native Peruvian habitat, Eve's Pin produces many angular, outward-pointing, pin-like leaves from its shrub-like body.

Eve's Pin

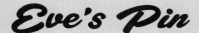

AUSTROCYLINDROPUNTIA SUBULATA

LIGHT:

Eve's Pin will grow in places with plenty of sunlight or in partial shade, and will thrive in an airy kitchen. Be aware, though, that while this plant enjoys some moisture, it needs adequate air circulation and very low humidity.

WATER:

Water moderately throughout the summer months once a week, but allow all the water to drain away so the pot dries out fully before the next watering. During winter make sure you only water just enough to prevent the leaves shrivelling.

GROWTH AND CARE:

The Eve's Pin is a tree-like cactus and if happy and regularly repotted it can grow up to 4m (13ft) tall, producing light yellow spines that can reach 15cm (6in) long. The plant produces red flowers in the summer, which are followed by red fruits.

PROPAGATION:

When propagating, cut the stem at the woody node where two branches meet. Wait for the cutting to crust over, then place in a loose, gritty soil for it to root.

Copper Pinwheels are native to the Canary Islands; however, they are now spotted as far away as California. Their leaves are a beautiful mix of bright greens and yellows with a faint pink outline that appears in the summer months, along with a delicate white flower from the centre of the crest.

Copper Pinwheel

AEONIUM DECORUM 'SUNBURST'

LIGHT: As the name suggests, this slow-growing succulent requires full sunlight or bright shade and temperatures no lower than -1°C (30°F). It is susceptible to frost damage, so keep your plant in a warm, sunny spot in your home and you will have success.

WATER: Water regularly during the summer months from April to October, but remember to let the soil dry out between waterings to prevent root rot.

GROWTH AND CARE: The Copper Pinwheel is a great container plant and can grow up to 46cm (18in) tall and wide. Their large rosettes are held on long bare stems and mature plants produce pale yellow flowers in early spring.

WATCH OUT FOR: Unfortunately, the Copper Pinwheel is fairly prone to stem and root rot, even if you keep the soil mostly dry. If the roots start to rot, slice off the top end of the root and place it in the soil to root again.

The origin of this cactus' name is clear. The bulbous, mutant-like form of the *Cereus* could have come straight out of a horror movie. With a tight bunch of twisted limbs and irregular growing patterns, many of these plants can look completely different from one another.

Monstrose Cactus

CEREUS HILMANNIANUS MONSTROSE

LIGHT: Plenty of sunlight will help you grow a tall strong cactus, but beware of leaving it in direct sunlight; a mixture of sunshine and shade is perfect.

WATER: In the summer water it once a week, allowing the soil to dry out completely between waterings. However, during the winter months it is important that you do not water it at all and make sure that the plant is not placed somewhere with high humidity such as a bathroom. Take care when watering, as if the plant is given too much water and shade it can become swollen and untidy.

POTTING: A very fast-growing cactus, this plant may need repotting every year. It can grow up to 20cm (8in) in height annually.

WATCH OUT FOR: In poorly draining soil this cactus can be prone to root rot. To avoid this buy some gravel or small stones from your local garden centre to place beneath the soil.

Native to South Africa, the String of Hearts is the ideal plant for your hanging baskets. Although the foliage is sparse, the focus here is on the dainty heart-shaped leaves, which cascade down the wiry stems.

String of Hearts

CEROPEGIA WOODII

LIGHT: This pretty plant, though needing minimal care, does require lots of light. When positioning the String of Hearts in your home be sure to place it in the sunniest room.

WATER: When in growth, water moderately but allow the compost to dry out completely between waterings. The roots and stems are delicate, so it is common for these plants to be overwatered. Yellowing leaves can be a good indication of root rot or low temperatures.

FLOWERS: This evergreen perennial will possibly flower during the summer months, producing quite nondescript pale-white flowers that will occasionally be followed by cylindrical fruit-bearing seeds.

PRUNING: This long-living vine is prone to getting a bit leggy over time and will benefit from a occasional haircut. You can then propagate any cuttings by inserting the cut ends back into moist soil.

Related to the more popular *Aeonium haworthii*, the *volkerii* is a tree-like *Aeonium*. It will offset readily and may quickly become a shrubby plant, with mainly green leaves and a red tinge to the edges that increases with exposure to sunlight.

Tree Aeonium

AEONIUM VOLKERII

LIGHT:

The growing season for this plant is from late winter to spring, during which time they should be kept in a moist, shady position.

WATER:

Aeoniums do not do well in very hot, dry environments; you may notice the leaves curling if they get too hot. This is a response by the plant to prevent water loss, an indication that your *Aeonium* needs a little water. During the winter months, *Aeoniums* should only be watered when the compost has completely dried out.

POTTING:

Consider growing the Tree Aeonium with other plants as they do well in communal, shallow pots as part of a group. Combine them with Aloe, Agave or Jade plants.

WATCH OUT FOR:

Although caring for *Aeoniums* is easy, be careful as this plant is prone to stem and root rot. This can be prevented if you use a clay pot with good drainage.

Endemic to South Africa, *Crassula arborescens* is usually found in the wild as a medium-sized shrub or small tree. Grown in the home, the Silver Dollar Plant - so-called because its leaves can grow to the size of a silver dollar - is just as happy in a small pot with ample sunlight. With blue-green leaves covered in tiny reddish-pink spots, the Silver Dollar Plant is one of the more attractive succulents.

Silver Dollar Plant

CRASSULA ARBORESCENS

LIGHT:

The Silver Dollar Plant will thrive in bright light with some direct sunlight. A bright windowsill would be perfect for this plant and will encourage flowering. Without sufficient light you may find your plant becomes spindly.

WATER:

Known to be drought tolerant, the Silver Dollar Plant can withstand serious bouts of neglect, but to help your plant to look its best, it is advisable to water once a week during the summer months and less frequently during cooler months.

FLOWERS:

During the summer, this plant produces a spectacular show of star-shaped flowers, appearing in small, ball-shaped clusters that dry out as small red balls on the ends of the leaves.

Perhaps one of the most attractive *Echeveria* with its fleshy lilac leaves, the Perle of Nürnberg can offset to form a clump of beautiful purple-blue rosettes that can each grow up to 30cm (12in) in diameter.

Pearl of Nürnberg

ECHEVERIA 'PERLE VON NÜRNBERG'

LIGHT:

This adaptable plant prefers high amounts of sunshine but also appreciates a bit of afternoon shade. In the summer months it can be left outdoors as long as the temperatures stay mildly warm.

WATER:

During warmer months, water well. Watering from below is the best way to prevent any build-up of water on the concave leaf structures that could lead to rotting or scarring. Do not allow the *Echeveria* to sit in a pot of water for long, as this can cause root rot. Water much more sparingly during the winter, allowing the soil to dry out completely between watering.

FLOWERS:

This *Echeveria* is unique in the number of flower stems that it may produce at one time. Up to six stems may branch out of one rosette, producing coral-orange flowers from late spring to early summer.

With its bright-green fleshy leaves, the Green Echeveria is a hardy succulent that grows well in most conditions. This Mexican native tolerates extremes of hot and cold. Most commonly, the plant features small, compact rosettes; however, the stems will sometimes grow towards the sunlight, producing offsets.

Green Echeveria ECHEVERIA AFFINIS

LIGHT: Green Echeverias enjoy the warmth of the sun, so allow yours a few hours of direct sunlight each day. This will encourage flowering, but watch out for any browning of the leaves. If this happens, immediately move your plant out of direct sunlight, especially during the hotter summer months.

WATER: This plant needs regular watering throughout the growing summer months. Only water once the soil has dried out completely, which should be about once a week. Throughout the winter keep watering to a minimum, as *Echeverias* can be susceptible to root rot. If indoors, the pot should not be allowed to stand in water.

FLOWERS: Flowering occurs late summer to early autumn. Long, arching stems will branch out from beneath the rosettes, producing an abundance of white flowers.

PROPAGATION: You can easily propagate from leaf cuttings. For the best results grow your plants from seeds or stem cuttings.

It is immediately apparent why this plant was given the name Old Man Cactus: the wispy white hairs that protrude from every surface of *Oreocereus trollii* resemble the thinning hair of an elderly man. Originating in the arid mountainous areas of Argentina, the hairs lining the cactus protect it from both late-night winter frosts and the intense summer sunshine at high altitudes.

Old Man Cactus

OREOCEREUS TROLLII

LIGHT:

Bright sunlight will allow the Old Man Cactus to reach its full potential. It is sensitive to humidity, so be sure to place it in an airy room with low humidity.

WATER:

In summer, water once a week only when the soil has dried out completely. In the cooler winter months refrain from watering at all while the cactus is dormant.

GROWTH AND CARE:

You may find that your Old Man Cactus picks up pieces of dust or dirt in its white hair. If this happens remove by brushing it off gently using a dry paintbrush.

POTTING:

Because it is a long, tubular cactus that quickly branches to clump at the base, you may need to repot your Old Man once every two years. Repot in spring and allow one or two weeks before watering.

There are more than 600 different species in the *Agave* genus and the most popular is known as the **Century Plant**, thought to flower only once every hundred years. With tall, pointy leaves, the Century Plant will quite often have white speckles on its edges.

 AGAVE AMERICANA

LIGHT:

As a desert native, an *Agave* will tolerate drought as well as appreciating a lot of sunlight – so much so that it will flourish if moved outside during the summer months.

WATER:

Easy to cultivate, *Agaves* are happy in any compost as long as it is free draining. Water them moderately once a week, allowing the compost to dry out completely between waterings to avoid root rot.

POTTING:

Agaves do best in soil with lots of grit. You can add grit through the soil to assist with filtering.

FLOWERS:

The *Agave's* rosettes die off after flowering, although this may take many years. They then leave space for a pup to take over.

WATCH OUT FOR:

Be aware that some species have sharp, serrated teeth along the edges of the leaves and can be midly toxic to cats and dogs.

Despite its tube-like stems that resemble hunting horns, this plant is closely related to the more common Jade Plant. This means that the Horn Tree can be cared for in much the same way as the Jade.

Developing a trunk that grows thick with age, this is an interesting plant to watch mature over time. It can grow up to 80cm (31.5in) high and 30cm (12in) in diameter, and can also be carefully sculpted to create an irregular bonsai plant.

Horn Tree   CRASSULA OVATA 'GOLLUM'

LIGHT:
This trumpet-like plant grows happily indoors in full sun; however, it will tolerate partial sun as well. Try to give your plant a few hours of natural sunshine every day to keep it happy.

WATER:
Throughout the summer water moderately, but make sure that the compost dries out completely before watering again. Do not overwater, especially in winter, when the plant can survive for a few weeks without any water at all.

GROWTH AND CARE:
A very fast-growing plant, young Horn Trees may quadruple in size in a year. When the roots start to outgrow the pot it is time to repot.

PROPAGATION:
Propagation can be easily achieved from leaf and stem cuttings. Fallen leaves will also self-sow at the base of the plant, rooting quickly in dry compost.

The Topsy Turvy has rosette-forming leaves which range from light blue-green to white-blue in colour. It is easily recognized by its U-shaped leaf pattern. One of the most unusual members of the *Echeveria* genus, it looks almost as though the leaves have been turned inside out.

Topsy Turvy

ECHEVERIA RUNYONII

WATER:

When watering this succulent, make sure that water does not accumulate in the leaf pockets. Its leaf shape makes the Topsy Turvy susceptible to rot and fungal diseases. As with most succulents, ample sunlight will encourage strong growth and colouring in both leaves and flowers.

GROWTH AND CARE:

This fast-growing succulent can grow rosettes of up to 25cm (10in) in diameter with silvery-grey leaves which grow up to 12.5cm (5in) long and 2.5cm (1in) wide.

FLOWERS:

A native of Mexico, the Topsy Turvy flowers appear quite spectacularly from one tall, arching raceme, showing bright yellow and orange blooms.

WATCH OUT FOR:

As the plant grows, remove any dead leaves from the bottom of the pot as they can be a haven for pests (*Echeveria* are particularly prone to mealy bugs) and this can be detrimental to the plant.

With a recognizable bright-blue patterned stem and contrasting yellow spines, the Tree Cactus is one of the most attractive cacti that can be grown indoors.

Tree Cactus PILOSOCEREUS AZUREUS

LIGHT:

Native to Mexico and Brazil, the Tree Cactus enjoys bright sunshine, but appreciates periods of shade as well, which promote the growth of its blue tubular flowers. These will eventually die back to produce spherical fruits.

WATER:

Tree Cacti need regular watering throughout the summer. Watering your plant thoroughly once a week should be sufficient, but make sure that the water can freely drain so that the roots do not sit in damp soil, as this can promote root rot. These cacti also benefit if given fertilizer throughout the summer in order for them to reach their full potential.

POTTING:

A Tree Cactus can grow to be 4.3m (14ft) tall and will benefit from sporadic repotting. Wear gloves, gently lift the plant from its pot, knock away the old soil and replant in a larger one.

PROPAGATION:

The best way to propagate a Tree Cactus is by taking a cutting. Just cut the top off a mature plant, then repot it as the bottom of a new one. It should take a few weeks, but will eventually fully root.

Grown for its elaborate leaf structure, the Fishbone Cactus can be identified by the zigzag pattern of its leaves protruding from a central spine. When dangling from a hanging basket, this plant could be straight from a Matisse painting.

Fishbone Cactus

EPIPHYLLUM ANGULIGER

LIGHT:
They like indirect sunlight, so a living room or bathroom is the perfect home for a Fishbone Cactus.

WATER:
A Fishbone Cactus appreciates regular watering, but avoid overwatering. Make sure that the compost is kept damp at all times; a humid environment is perfect for this jungle plant.

FLOWERS:
As a member of the night-blooming cactus family, the Fishbone very occasionally produces small pink flowers that open overnight and last for only one day. If you're lucky enough to witness this spectacular vision, enjoy the moment.

WATCH OUT FOR:
Although there are no visible spines, take care when handling a Fishbone Cactus as millions of tiny hairs line the stems; when touched, they can cause some irritation and discomfort.

This is a small, slow-growing *Echeveria* with dark, mottled, olive-green leaves, sometimes with a red-brown tinge. The pointy leaves come together to form a tight rosette that can grow up to 8cm (3in) in diameter. Usually a solitary plant, you may find that in the right conditions your *Echeveria* will offset and start to form a dense clump; the pups can always be repotted when rooted.

ECHEVERIA PURPUSORUM

LIGHT: Ample sunlight and a warm spot will be the perfect environment for your *Echeveria purpusorum*. Sun and heat will increase the intensity of the red colour on the leaves and promote flowering. Be sure not to leave it in direct sunlight, as this can scald your plant.

WATER: When watering your *Echeveria* do not allow water to sit on the rosettes, as this can cause rotting or lead to a potentially fatal fungal infection.

GROWTH AND CARE: As your plant grows you will start to see an accumulation of dead leaves at the bottom. It is important to remove these as soon as possible as they can be the perfect home for small pests such as the mealy bug.

FLOWERS: The red-orange flowers sprout from a curved stem that can grow to be 20cm (8in) tall.

A low, creeping succulent with small, fleshy red and green leaves, the Calico Kitten is often found as thick vegetation covering rocks and ravines in its native South Africa. If you have a rock garden at home, this *Crassula* will be happy there. Alternatively it will also thrive in a hanging pot which allows its spindly limbs to flow freely downwards.

#

CRASSULA PELLUCIDA RUBRA

LIGHT: This plant's leaf colour changes depending on how much sun it receives. Sunlight starts to turn the leaves a red colour, which can look quite attractive, but be aware that the Calico Kitten enjoys shade as well.

WATER: The Calico Kitten requires little or no maintenance – a splash of water every week or so will be enough to keep the leaves succulent and healthy. Be careful not to overwater it as this ground-covering plant can rot easily.

FLOWERS: If given enough sun during springtime, this *Crassula* may produce tiny star-like white flowers. Although relatively unimpressive, they do add to the plant's attractiveness. However, once the flowers have died off, the plant may deteriorate slightly. This can be a good opportunity to tidy up and trim back long stems.

It is easy to see why the *Euphorbia lactea* is also known as the Coral Cactus. With its erect spine and fan-like coral-pink oceanic branches, this plant is widely grown as an ornamental houseplant.

Coral Cactus EUPHORBIA LACTEA

LIGHT: Placed in a bright, sunny position, this plant will thrive on a windowsill in normal indoor temperatures.

WATER: Although it is not a cactus, the Coral Cactus can be treated in much the same way as one; water minimally in winter and once a week in summer.

POTTING: You only need to repot your Coral Cactus every four years. Repot in spring or early summer in a pot 2cm (3/4in) larger than the original.

WATCH OUT FOR: Be careful when handling the Coral Cactus. It is used medicinally in India, but like most *Euphorbia*, when its spines are broken off, the Coral Cactus produces a toxic white mucus, which can cause skin irritation and hallucinations. This plant is also toxic to cats and dogs.

QUIRKS: This species is not created by a cactus, but is two succulents grafting together: *Euphorbia lactea* being the fan-like crest which is grafted on to *Euphorbia neriifolia* rootstock.

This small, shrub-like plant has serrated green-brown oval leaves that increase their red tones in response to drought, the cold or warm sun.

Kalanchoe Longiflora

KALANCHOE LONGIFLORA

LIGHT:

Sunlight is important to keep the plant's strength up. Ideally place your *Kalanchoe longiflora* on a window ledge or somewhere with ample direct sunlight. Some light afternoon shade, however, is also welcome, and will increase the chance of flowering.

WATER:

When watering, ensure that the soil is left to dry out completely before adding more, as too much water can cause root rot. Water once a week during the summer months, then once every few weeks in the winter.

GROWTH AND CARE:

Make sure you pot your plant with plenty of grit or sand in the soil as the *Kalanchoe longiflora* thrives given good air circulation and free drainage around its root system.

FLOWERS:

Canary-yellow flowers bloom from tall spikes during the late spring and early summer. Trim off the flowers once they have bloomed.

Resembling an English shrub rather than a desert cactus, the Crown of Thorns grows fast into a dense, multi-branched plant that can easily get out of hand and resemble a tangled mess.

Crown of Thorns EUPHORBIA MILII

POTTING: Your Crown of Thorns will need repotting every two years in late winter or early spring. Use well-drained soil and transfer to a pot that will accommodate the roots comfortably without squashing them.

FLOWERS: Flowers are small and often bright red or pink in colour. Usually quite nondescript, the Crown of Thorns can look impressive when in full bloom and is a favourite flower houseplant.

WATCH OUT FOR: The sap is relatively poisonous, and can cause skin irritation and burning. This plant can also be toxic to pets so keep it out of reach of dogs and cats.

QUIRKS: Native to Madagascar this *Euphorbia* keeps its leaves far longer than any other plant in this genus. It eventually sheds them all, leaving only the sharp thorns that line each stem.

DID YOU KNOW: The Crown of Thorns is also known as the Christ Plant.

A cactus without a spine, the Bunny Ears is made up of pad-like leaves, which are covered with tiny clusters of spines called glochids; these are thinner than human hairs. However, because they are so fine, they can cause severe skin irritation even if they feel painless to touch. The Bunny Ears is one of the most popular cacti in cultivation because the plants remain small and shrub-like for many years.

Bunny Ears Cactus

OPUNTIA MICRODASYS 'ALBATA'

LIGHT: Used to the bright sun of the desert, the Bunny Ears Cactus grows well on a window ledge or in a greenhouse. Do not keep it in direct sunlight for too long, as this may burn the skin of the cactus.

WATER: During the summer months water your *Opuntia* once a week, allowing the soil to dry out completely between waterings. In winter this cacti is very resilient, preferring cooler temperatures; it can go without water for weeks at a time, so only water it enough to prevent the leaves from shrivelling.

FLOWERS: Flowers are relatively rare. However, if your plant does flower it will produce bright yellowish-orange flowers on the edges of the leaf pads. These will be followed by red fruit.

An evergreen creeping perennial, the Cape Blanco will only reach heights of about 10cm (4in). If planted in a pot it will slowly create a carpet of grey-purple rosettes and looks lovely in a hanging basket with its stems hanging over the sides.

Cape Blanco

SEDUM SPATHULIFOLIUM

LIGHT:

This stonecrop enjoys full sunlight which will increase the vibrancy of the purple leaves. It will be happy on a sunny window ledge or outside in the warmer summer months. During winter, it will not survive the frost, so be sure to bring it inside.

WATER:

Do not allow it to sit in damp soil. Keep watering to a minimum during the winter period, as the plant will be in a state of dormancy. As it becomes warmer from spring through summer only water once a week, ensuring that the plant is in a free-draining soil that will not retain any moisture.

FLOWERS:

Cape Blanco will flower from late summer to early autumn when clusters of small, yellow, star-shaped flowers mingle with the bed of rosettes.

DID YOU KNOW:

?

The Cape Blanco is also known as the Spoon-leaved Stonecrop.

Euphorbias come in many different forms; the *tirucalli* genus is native to northern Africa, and will sit happily in a pot on your shelf at home. However, in its natural arid habitat this plant can grow into a tree up to 3m (10ft) tall.

Pencil Cactus

EUPHORBIA TIRUCALLI

WATER:

The Pencil Cactus needs regular watering throughout the summer months; just make sure the compost dries out fully between waterings. As the plant becomes dormant in the winter months you will only need to water once every few weeks.

WATCH OUT FOR:

This plant is also moderately poisonous to cats and dogs if ingested so be wary for your pet if you keep your plant on the floor.

QUIRKS:

The stems of these plants are usually smooth and green, only turning grey as the plant starts to age. Look for the vibrant Sticks on Fire or Red Pencil Tree as their stems have attractive bright-red tips that respond to heat, gaining intensity in colour as the temperature rises, then fading as it cools.

DID YOU KNOW:

The Pencil Cactus is known as a leafless cactus. Its many pencil-shaped stems have taken over the role of leaves.

This succulent can be found in the eastern cape of South Africa. A dense *Haworthia*, it is formed of hundreds of pointy blue-green stems that are packed tightly to form long clumps.

Haworthia Glauca var. Herrei

HAWORTHIA GLAUCA VAR. HERREI

LIGHT:
Found hiding under the desert shrubs, at home a *Haworthia Glauca* will thrive in a lot of natural light with intermittent shade. Keep on a window ledge, or – better still – in a greenhouse for strong growth and a healthy plant.

WATER:
Unlike most succulents this *Haworthia* is a winter grower and lies dormant during the summer months. During summer you will need to keep the soil moist but not soaked; during winter decrease watering to a few times a month and only water to prevent the leaves from shrivelling when the compost is dry.

PROPAGATION:
This plant can be easily propagated by separating its offsets and replanting them. You can also grow the *Haworthia Glauca* from the seed.

QUIRKS:
These plants have the ability to change colour. Cooler winter weather will bring a red-orange hue to the rosettes.

Native to the Cape of South Africa, this *Gasteria* is made up of two fans of tongue-shaped dark-green leaves. The name *Verrucosa* means rough and warty; and describes the texture of the leaves.

 **Ox Tongue** GASTERIA VERRUCOSA

LIGHT:

Enjoying large amounts of sunlight, this succulent will do very well in a bright and airy room, and will be even happier on a windowsill, although do make sure that it isn't exposed to direct sunlight all day as this will burn the leaves. The sunlight will encourage the blooming of the orange and red flowers that can appear throughout the late summer and early autumn.

WATER:

Tolerant of neglect, the Ox Tongue can go for long periods without water, although it will appreciate a weekly sprinkling, especially in the summer months. During winter you can leave many weeks between waterings. Ensure that the plant is in a free-draining, gritty soil.

PROPAGATION:

Left alone, the Ox Tongue will form large clusters, sprouting pups from the base of the original plant. These can be left to grow or used to easily propagate a new plant.

DID YOU KNOW:

The Ox Tongue is also known as the Tongue Aloe and Warted Aloe.

The beautiful blue-minty green coloured leaves of Blue Hens and Chicks make it a favourite little succulent to have in your home.

Blue Hens and Chicks

ECHEVERIA SECUNDA VAR. GLAUCA

LIGHT:
This *Echeveria* will be happy in full sunshine or partial shade. Just make sure that water droplets don't gather on the concave leaves, as in bright sunshine this can cause browning and discolouration.

WATER:
Water moderately in the summer months, allowing the compost to dry out between waterings. However, in the winter the compost should be kept almost completely dry, so only water enough to prevent the fleshy leaves shrivelling.

FLOWERS:
During the summer growing season, Blue Hens and Chicks may produce a single spike of bright-pink bell-shaped flowers. When this dies back the rosette will die as well, leaving room for a new offset to take its place.

PROPAGATION:
Blue Hens and Chicks can be propagated using leaf cuttings. Gently pull a lower leaf from the rosette and leave it on a bed of dry compost to callus over. When the leaf has started to root, you can plant it in a dry and gritty compost.

This succulent is small in size and can grow to be 10cm (4in) tall. A showy, clumping cactus with white spines and vibrant yellow flowers that bloom throughout the summer months, the *Coryphantha sulcata* originates from Texas and has evolved to tolerate intense sunshine, and long periods of drought.

Pineapple Cactus

CORYPHANTHA SULCATA

LIGHT:

Place the Pineapple Cactus where it will receive large amounts of direct sunshine. Insufficient light will cause the body of the cactus to lose its vibrant green colour and turn a paler shade of yellowy brown. Increasing the amount of sunshine will encourage flowers and increase the chance of flowering the following year.

WATER:

The Pineapple Cactus needs minimal watering through the warmer summer months; once every few weeks should be sufficient. Decrease watering during the cold winter months, ensuring that the soil is kept as dry as possible. Water just enough to prevent the protruding nipples of the plant shrivelling. Although this cactus is frost tolerant bring it inside during the colder months to protect it from the rain. Prolonged exposure to damp can cause root rot, which can be potentially fatal to the *Coryphantha sulcata*.

Known as a leaf succulent because of its apparent lack of a central stem, the Stone Plant is an alien-looking plant with a single pair of fleshy leaves that fuse underground, then slightly separate around a gouge on the surface. The plant is small and button-shaped, with a completely flat surface.

 **Stone Plant** LITHOPS OLIVACEA

WATER: The Stone Plant is relatively easy to keep at home and only requires water once a week most of the year, but it needs special care during its yearly shedding. Every year the leaf pair is replaced by a new one while the old one shrivels around it, but for this to happen the soil must be kept completely dry from the end of the flowering season (early winter) until the new leaves have fully developed in early summer. Watering during this time will not prove fatal; however, it will encourage rapid growth by the plant and extra leaves may develop, so the plant loses its two-leaf, pebble-like appearance.

QUIRKS: In their native South Africa, Stone Plants are often mistaken for pinkish-brown stones or pebbles as they grow as clumps on the ground. The plants have a window on the top of each leaf, allowing sunlight to reach the lower area of the leaf underground.

DID YOU KNOW: The Stone Plant is also known as Living Stones.

With an appearance that is almost Jurassic, the *Kalanchoe laetivirens* is a perennial succulent with fleshy green-grey leaves that offset many smaller leaves - hence the name Mother of Thousands. The undersides of the leaves have a purple-brown camouflage pattern that contrasts beautifully with their bright-green tops.

Mother of Thousands

KALANCHOE LAETIVIRENS

LIGHT: The Mother of Thousands prefers moderate sunlight with small amounts of shade. Do not allow it to sit in direct sunlight, however, as this can scald and damage the leaves.

WATER: During the summer growing months, the Mother of Thousands will need plenty of water to ensure strong growth and succulent, fleshy leaves. As the weather cools in the winter, decrease watering to once every few weeks and ensure that the soil dries out fully in between waterings to prevent root rot.

FLOWERS: During late winter or early spring, the Mother of Thousands will shoot up a tall spike of showy pink bell-shaped flowers.

WATCH OUT FOR Mother of Thousands, like other *Kalanchoe*; is poisonous to cats and dogs when ingested.

One of the most common houseplants, the Hairy Stemmed Rhipsalis is known for its long, rope-like stems that grow from the centre. Used to growing epiphytically in its natural environment, your Hairy Stemmed Rhipsalis will be content hanging from a basket with enough room for its trailing limbs to grow.

Hairy Stemmed Rhipsalis

RHIPSALIS PILOCARPA

LIGHT:

Rhipsalis pilocarpa thrives in indirect sunlight in the morning with full afternoon shade. However, this plant is quite sensitive to light and exposure to direct sunlight, which can burn the leaves or even stunt its growth.

WATER:

Endemic to the rainforests of South America, this jungle cactus needs watering regularly. Over-watering, however, can cause root rot and weaken the plant's stems. Check the soil before watering by pressing your finger on the top of the soil to see if its moist. Only water when the soil is dry.

FLOWERS:

The Hairy Stemmed Rhipsalis produces pale pink flowers that bloom in the autumn or early winter, when the plant is mature. These flowers can last for several days.

POTTING:

The Hairy Stemmed Rhipsalis prefers to grow in a clay pot, as this will allow the soil to breathe and prevent root rot. The clay will also dissipate moisture.

An erect plant with green, tongue-shaped, leathery leaves with a yellow stripe, the Mother-in-Law's Tongue has become a popular houseplant due to its air-purifying capabilities. The plant spreads by a means of underground rhizomes, and when kept in a pot soon produces a dense clump of leaves.

Mother-in-Law's Tongue
SANSEVERIA TRIFASCIATA

LIGHT:

The Mother-in-Law's Tongue is certainly a sun-worshipper, and you will rapidly start to see the effects of light deprivation if it is kept in darkness for any length of time.

WATER:

Positively thriving on neglect, this Central African plant can go weeks without water. However, high humidity can be damaging, so it will prefer sitting on a windowsill to being kept in a greenhouse.

FLOWERS:

Although the *Sanseveria trifasciata* is relatively easy to look after, it does not flower when kept as a house plant.

PROPAGATION:

The Mother-in-Law's Tongue can be propagated by taking leaf cuttings, planting the ends closest to the underground rhizomes.

DID YOU KNOW:

In the past this plant had many uses, one of which was producing a strong plant fibre known as bowstring hemp.

The Prickly Pear Cactus is native to eastern parts of North America. This thorny plant gained its name from the large, oval-shaped, often edible yellow-and-red fruits it produces.

Eastern Prickly Pear

OPUNTIA VULGARIS

LIGHT:

As a desert cactus, the Prickly Pear should be kept in full sunlight whenever possible. Direct sunlight is highly beneficial to see your plant thrive.

WATER:

The Prickly Pear cactus only needs to be watered once the surface of its soil looks dry. On average during the spring and summer, you need to water your plant once or twice a week. In autumn and winter your plant will require water once or twice a month.

GROWTH AND CARE:

This cactus is easy to grow but needs well-drained, sandy and loamy soil. Try to avoid clay-rich soil that retains moisture.

PROPAGATION:

Prickly Pears can be easily propagated by taking a cutting. If you sever a limb of the cactus and leave it until the cut has dried out, it can be placed on a bed of gritty soil until it starts to root. Do not water until rooting has begun or the cutting may start to rot.

This creeping perennial can be recognized by its small, pea-sized leaves, which lace its trailing vines like a pearl necklace. Native to the drier parts of south-west Africa, the String of Pearls is found draped over branches and falling to the ground in clusters, but in the home it will be content in a hanging basket.

String of Pearls

SENECIO ROWLEYANUS

LIGHT:

The String of Pearls will grow happily in bright sunlight at room temperature, but do not expose the plant to too much humidity, as this can cause root rot, especially if there is not sufficient drainage.

WATER:

The plant's ability to store water in its leaves means that it can be thoroughly watered one week, then left unattended for the next few. Allow the soil to dry out completely before you water again.

FLOWERS:

The String of Pearls rarely flowers in the home. If yours does you will see pale-white flowers that smell faintly of cinnamon.

PRUNING:

You may have to prune your String of Pearls, as the vines can sometimes become tangled and unruly. Trim off any dead pearls and trim back vines that have lost their leaves; this will help your plant become fuller and happier.

A native of various regions in Mexico and a member of the stonecrops, the large, succulent lobes of the Moonstones plant clump together and look like a collection of white pebbles. Found as a small shrub under the shade of larger plants, this small succulent will be happy in a small window-positioned pot.

Moonstones PACHYPHYTUM BRACTEOSUM

LIGHT: Moonstones grow well in full sun, with partial shade to protect it from any direct sunlight. Conditions should be dry and arid.

WATER: When watering, make sure water does not collect on the leaves, as it can mark the silvery surface and cause rot. In spring and summer you will need to water your Moonstones once a week, allowing the soil to dry out between waterings. During winter, decrease watering to once every few weeks, and only water enough to prevent the leaves from shrivelling.

GROWTH AND CARE: Moonstones are one of the simplest succulents to care for: generally disease-free, this pebble-like plant should require no pruning apart from the occasional removal of dead leaves.

FLOWERS: During spring, this succulent will flower producing rose-pink buds from an arching stalk in the centre of the rosette. Ample sunlight will increase the vibrancy of the blooms.

Native to Belgium but hardy in the English countryside, you will find the *Sempervivum* 'passionata' forming large clumps between rocks and in crevices. Its vibrant rosettes of slender leaves in a multitude of rich, red colours make this plant a welcome addition to any succulent collection in the home.

Hen and Chicks

SEMPERVIVUM 'PASSIONATA'

LIGHT:
Keep it in indirect sunlight and your *Sempervivum* will thrive.

WATER:
Water sparingly: once a week during the summer months, then less frequently in the winter.

PROPAGATION:
The Hen and Chicks can be easily propagated. Simply remove the plant's offsets in the spring or early summer and place each individual chick in a pot of soil of its own. You can also propagate this plant from its seed, which needs to be sown in early spring where they will on average take about two to six weeks to germinate.

DID YOU KNOW:
The large parent rosette of the *Sempervivum* 'passionata' is known as the hen, while the little offsets are the chicks which is where the plant gets its common name from.

Originating in southern China, it is easy to see why this plant is also known as the Pancake Plant. Its easily recognizable round, flat leaves make it a focal plant in your home, especially as its structured leaves contrast well with those of most plants its size.

Chinese Money Plant

PILEA PEPEROMIOIDES

LIGHT: Growing to only about 30cm (12in) high, these beauties are partial to a shady spot, so they grow well on a windowsill in the winter. However, don't put this plant in direct sunlight as this might damage its leaves.

WATER: Relatively easy to care for, the Chinese Money Plant is happy in free-draining soil and will enjoy being watered once a week when the soil has completely dried out, possibly more often during the hot summer months.

PROPAGATION: Chinese Money Plants produce many pups that sprout out of the base of the mother plant. These can be removed and propagated in a new pot very easily.

DID YOU KNOW: A relatively new plant, the *Pilea peperomioides* was discovered in 1906, then lost again until the 1940s, when it was distributed via cuttings among amateur gardeners before becoming well known to botanists.

Growing around 400m (1,312ft) above sea level in the Amazonian region of Peru, the *Matucana madisoniorum* is often found as a solid, globular mass. Some are completely without spines; others have a few lone spines dotted over the surface.

Matucana madisoniorum

MATUCANA MADISONIORUM

LIGHT:
A slow grower in its natural habitat, the *Matucana* will grow much faster in a greenhouse, but avoid exposing it to long periods of direct sunlight, as this can burn the plant, leaving unattractive markings on its body.

WATER:
Matucanas thrive in rich, porous soil but be sure to allow the soil to dry out completely between waterings, which in summer should be done sparingly once a week and in winter even less frequently.

POTTING:
Repot in spring, when the roots become cramped and the plant is relatively dormant. Fresh soil will help to promote new growth, but after repotting do not water the plant for about two weeks.

FLOWERS:
Flowering multiple times during one growing season, the *Matucana madisoniorum*'s bright-red or orange flowers can arch up to 10cm (4in) long and 3.5cm (1¼in) in diameter, and are sometimes much wider than the actual cactus.

A native of the bush regions of Kenya, the woody leaves of the Walking Sansevieria fan out to produce a plaited pattern along the central stem of the plant. Plant it in a porous and gritty soil mix.

Walking Sansevieria

SANSEVIERIA PINGUICULA

LIGHT:

Most *Sansevierias* will survive in a wide range of light conditions, but the *pinguicula* will thrive in bright direct sunlight as well as a shady corner, as long as it receives a few hours of indirect sunlight every day.

WATER:

When watering, ensure that the compost is allowed to dry out completely before watering again; the Walking Sansevieria is highly susceptible to root rot. When the plant is sufficiently watered you will notice that the undersides of the leaves are long and smooth. However, in drier conditions you will start to notice long ridges developing on the underside as the plant draws on all its water supplies. During the summer months water once a week; during colder winter months decrease watering to once every few weeks.

FLOWERS:

The Walking Sansevieria produces flowers that are whitish to pale yellow-green; however, they are not known for their ornamental qualities.

A member of the *Crassulaceae* family, the **Coppertone** comes from Mexico, and boasts beautiful orange-copper coloured succulent leaves.

Coppertone Sedum

SEDUM NUSSBAUMERIANUM

LIGHT: Thriving on neglect, this sedum can survive intense sunlight and with very little water. In your home it should ideally be placed on a window ledge that gets a lot of morning sunlight but it also appreciates a little afternoon shade. Alternatively, Coppertones are also happy in a hanging basket that allows their limbs to hang over the side.

WATER: Keep watering to a minimum. Make sure the soil is kept dry and roots are not left in damp soil, as this could result in root rot. Water once a week during the summer months, allowing the soil to dry out completely between waterings. During the dormant winter months only water the succulent enough to stop the leaves shrivelling.

FLOWERS: The white spheres of flowers produced by the Coppertone are rare; they are one of the few succulent flowers that have a floral fragrance.

Covered in a hairy, cobwebby coating, it is clear how this succulent has earned its name. A native of the Pyrenees, the cobweb-like fur coating has developed as protection from the extreme heat and hard frosts that the plant survives. The centre of the rosettes is reminiscent of a spider's web.

Cobweb Houseleek

SEMPERVIVUM ARACHNOIDEUM

LIGHT:

The Cobweb Houseleek is most at home in full sunlight. A small pot on a kitchen windowsill will thrive as long as the humidity is low.

WATER:

Watering should be kept to a minimum and the soil should be left to dry out completely between waterings. The roots sit quite close to the surface, so press your finger on the top of the soil to test if it is moist. Water sparingly during the winter months and more frequently during the summer months.

PROPAGATION:

Like most *Sempervivum* the Cobweb Houseleek produces offsets which form small clumps. These can be removed and repotted to propagate.

Arid

An arid land or climate has little rain or moisture and is often too barren to support vegetation.

Callus

This is a process that occurs after a cutting is made and the wound is left to dry so the damaged tissues seal over, reducing the chance of a fungal attack.

Epiphytic

An epiphytic plant grows harmlessly upon another plant but derives nutrients and moisture from the air and the rain.

Germination

This is a process when a seed, in the right condition, sprouts and develops into a new plant.

Leggy

A plant that has long, spindly, often leafless stems. When this occurs you may find your plant produces fewer flowers and is prone to flopping over. To combat this make sure your plant gets adequate light, and prune it back to encourage thicker growth.

Offset

An offset is a small new plant that is naturally produced by the parent plant, which can be propagated.

Pups

A plant that develops as an offset from a parent plant.

Raceme

This is a flower cluster attached to a central axis with separate flowers attached by short stalks at equal distances along the stem.

Rhizome

This is when a horizontal plant stem, usually situated underground, produces the shoot and root systems of a new plant. Rhizome is also called creeping rootstalk.

Spindly

A tall and thin plant. This can be unattractive and can weaken the plant. Solve the problem by pruning the spindly end.

SUPPLIERS

The publisher wishes to thank the following suppliers for their generous loans of plants and pots for the book.

CONSERVATORY ARCHIVES
www.conservatoryarchives.com
A London mecca for all plant collectors

PRICK
www.prickldn.com
A cacti lover's paradise

NEW COVENT GARDEN MARKET
www.newcoventgardenmarket.com

SURREAL SUCCULENTS
www.surrealsucculents.co.uk

Having the perfect pot for your plants makes all the difference.

CONCRETE JUNGLE
www.concretejungles.co.uk/#cactus

CONPOT
www.conpot.co.uk

ELLA HOOKWAY
www.ellahookway.com

**HARRIET LEVY-COOPER /
LAZY GLAZE**
www.lazyglaze.co.uk

LOUISE MADZIA
www.louisemadzia.com

**MELISSA GRACE FRANIE /
EL-AICH DESIGNS**
www.etsy.com/uk/people/
melissagrace5050

ORNAMENTAL GRACE
www.ornamentalgrace.co.uk

SMUG
www.ifeelsmug.com

LONDON TERRARIUMS

www.londonterrariums.com

ABOUT THE AUTHOR

Emma Sibley has had a keen interest in horticulture from a young age and after studying Surface Design at university, she changed career direction to work with plants. She took a number of short courses to increase her knowledge and love of all things green. Emma now runs a growing start-up business called London Terrariums and offers workshops, interior displays and private commissions. Emma is a member of the British Cactus and Succulent Society.

ACKNOWLEDGMENTS

I would like to thank all of the people who have helped us source the Cacti and Succulents, especially Gynelle from PRICK and Jin from Conservatory Archives, as well as all of the amazing ceramists that loaned your pots and planters for the shoot.

PUBLISHING DIRECTOR Sarah Lavelle
CREATIVE DIRECTOR Helen Lewis
EDITOR Harriet Butt
DESIGNER Gemma Hayden
PHOTOGRAPHER Adam Laycock
PROP STYLIST Holly Bruce
PRODUCTION DIRECTOR Vincent Smith
PRODUCTION CONTROLLER Emily Noto

First published in 2017 by Quadrille,
an imprint of Hardie Grant Publishing

Quadrille
52 Southwark Street
London SE1 1UN
quadrille.com

Reprinted in 2017 (four times), 2018 (three times), 2019
10 9

Text © 2017 Emma Sibley
Photography © 2017 Adam Laycock
Design and layout © 2017
Quadrille Publishing Limited

Cataloguing in Publication Data: a catalogue
record for this book is available from the
British Library.

ISBN 978 1 84949 914 9

Printed in China